COOK ME A RHYME

In the kitchen with Mother Goose

BY BRYAN KOZLOWSKI

ILLUSTRATED BY LAURA WOOD

TABLE OF CONTENTS

BEFORE THE RHYMES BEGIN...

Put on your aprons. Come on, everyone pitch in;
It's time for some fun in Mother Goose's kitchen!

There are pots to stir and tummies to fill,
And drinks to be made with Jack and Jill.

Humpty Dumpty's coming for brunch,
And we'll eat in the garden with Mary for lunch.

So get out your pans and open the cupboard,
Fetch all the food with Old Mother Hubbard.

Gather the flour, the sugar, and the juice,
And listen real careful to our Mother Goose.

She'll teach us to cook and bake just right,
She'll keep us safe from a kitchen fright.

For recipes are fun to make and learn,
But knives can cut and stoves can burn.

So look for Mother Goose's face,
When recipes come to a dangerous place.

That's your clue to ask for help,
Call for a grown-up, holler and yelp.

Do just that for a jolly good time,
Cooking your way through a nursery rhyme!

THIS IS THE WAY WE MAKE
OUR BRUNCH...

HUMPTY DUMPTY
Eggs in Tumbledown Toast

❀

BAA, BAA, BLACK SHEEP
Bag Full of Black Wool Granola

❀

LITTLE BOY BLUE
Blueberry Haystack Muffins

❀

PETER, PETER, PUMPKIN EATER
Pumpkin Drinker Juice

❀

PAT-A-CAKE
Mark it with a "B" Breakfast Cake

HUMPTY DUMPTY

EGGS IN TUMBLEDOWN TOAST

Serves Two

THIS RHYME NEEDS:

2 slices sandwich bread, preferably white

2 ounces (55 g) cubed ham, about ⅓ cup

2 eggs

Salt and pepper

½ cup (50 g) shredded Colby-Jack cheese

Preheat oven to 400°F (200°C)

Humpty Dumpty sat on a wall…

To make Humpty Dumpty's wall, place the bread on a nonstick baking tray. Using your fingers, press firmly down in the center of each slice to create a square-shaped well. Leave about a ½ inch (1.25 cm) of space around the well. Then, poke the ham cubes— the bricks—into the bread around the edge of the pressed-in well.

Humpty Dumpty had a great fall…

Crack one egg into each of the pressed-in centers of the bread slices. Lightly sprinkle each egg with salt and pepper.

All the king's horses and all the king's men...

Sprinkle the cheese over the ham cubes around the egg.

Couldn't put Humpty together again.

Put the baking tray into the oven, and cook for 10 to 12 minutes (depending on how soft you like your egg). Remove the tray from the oven with oven mitts, and transfer each Tumbledown Toast onto a plate using a spatula.

BAA, BAA, BLACK SHEEP

BAG FULL OF BLACK WOOL GRANOLA

Serves Four

THIS RHYME NEEDS:

¼ cup (23 g) cocoa powder
¼ cup (60 ml) vegetable oil
3 tablespoons honey
1 teaspoon vanilla extract
1 gallon-sized plastic resealable bag
2 cups (180 g) old-fashioned oats
¼ cup (57 g) packed dark brown sugar
Salt

Preheat oven to 300˚F (150˚C)

Baa, baa, black sheep, have you any wool?

Put the "black wool" cocoa powder, oil, honey, and vanilla extract into a small mixing bowl and stir until combined. Set the bowl aside.

Yes sir, yes sir, three bags full.

Open the plastic bag and pour the oats inside.

One for my master…

Add the brown sugar and a pinch of salt into the bag. Seal the bag closed and shake it until the sugar is mixed with the oats.

And one for the dame…

Open the bag and pour in the cocoa honey mixture. Close the bag tightly and shake it well until all the oats are coated in the mixture.

And one for the little boy who lives down the lane.

Open the bag and place the oats onto a nonstick (or parchment-lined) baking tray. Walk down the lane to the oven, and slide the tray inside to bake for 20 minutes.

Baa, baa, black sheep, have you any wool?
Yes sir, yes sir, three bags full.

Using oven mitts, remove the tray from the oven. Let the granola cool before breaking it into small clusters, and then store it in a resealable bag until ready to eat.

LITTLE BOY BLUE

BLUEBERRY HAYSTACK MUFFINS

Makes Twelve

THIS RHYME NEEDS:

Nonstick cooking spray
1 box (16.25 ounces / 461 g) white cake mix
1 cup (50 g) frosted cornflakes cereal
¾ cup (115 g) fresh blueberries
2 (5.3-ounce / 150 g) containers blueberry yogurt
⅔ cup (150 ml) water

Preheat oven to 350°F (180°C)

Little Boy Blue, come blow your horn...

*"Blow" non-stick cooking spray inside each cup of a 12-cup muffin tin.
Set the tin aside.*

The sheep's in the meadow...

*Put the white cake mix—the fluffy white sheep—
into a large mixing bowl and set it aside.*

15

The cow's in the corn.

Pour the cornflakes into a separate large bowl, and crush them to make large crumbs. Set aside.

But where is the boy who looks after the sheep?

Mix the fresh blueberries, blueberry yogurt, and water with the cake mix, stirring together until thick and blended (it's okay if the batter is lumpy). Spoon the batter into the muffin tin, filling each cup almost full.

He's under the haystack...

Sprinkle the cornflake crumbs—the "haystack"—over each mound of batter in the tin.

Fast asleep.

Place the muffin tin in the oven for 20 minutes or until the batter is set. Using oven mitts, remove the tin from the oven and let the muffins cool completely before eating. Shh...Little Boy Blueberries are sleeping.

PETER, PETER, PUMPKIN EATER

PUMPKIN
DRINKER JUICE
Makes Three Cups

THIS RHYME NEEDS:

½ cup (140 g) canned pumpkin puree
2½ cups (750 ml) apple juice
1 packed tablespoon dark brown sugar

Peter, Peter, Pumpkin eater…

Put the pumpkin puree, apple juice, and brown sugar into a large mixing bowl.

He had a wife but couldn't keep her…

Stir the juice with a whisk until the ingredients are well combined.

He put her in a pumpkin shell...

Using a ladle, pour the pumpkin juice through a wire sieve and into a pitcher.
Throw away the leftover pumpkin pulp.

And there he kept her very well.

Place the pitcher in the refrigerator to chill. Before you drink it, give it a quick stir. The pumpkin juice will keep "very well" in the refrigerator for one week.

PAT-A-CAKE

MARK IT WITH A "B"
BREAKFAST CAKE

Serves Six

THIS RHYME NEEDS:

2 (17.3 ounce/ 490 g) frozen puff pastry sheets, thawed
4 ounces (114 g) cream cheese, softened
2 teaspoons plus 3 tablespoons all-purpose flour
⅓ cup (110 g) raspberry jam
2 tablespoons water

 Preheat oven to 400°F (200°C)

Pat-a-cake, pat-a-cake…

Unfold the thawed puff pastry sheets on a cutting board and, one at a time, cut out an 8-inch (20 cm) circle from each sheet. Place one pastry round on a nonstick baking tray and set it aside.

Baker's man…

To make the baked-in filling, mix the softened cream cheese and sugar in a bowl with a spoon or electric mixer until combined. Add 2 teaspoons of flour and mix it into the cream cheese.

23

Bake me a cake, as fast as you can...

Spoon the cream cheese mixture onto the middle of the pastry round on the baking tray. Spread the cream cheese evenly with a butter knife, leaving about a 1-inch (2.5 cm) space around the edge of the pastry. Dot the raspberry jam onto the cream cheese and spread it evenly to the edge of the cream cheese.

Pat it...

Place the second pastry round over the first, covering the jam and cream cheese. Pat and press the edges of the two pastry rounds together with your fingers to make a thin, tight seal around the crust.

And prick it...

Using the tip of a small knife, poke about 20 tiny holes into the top of the cake.

And mark it with a B...

Stir the water and 3 tablespoons of flour in a small bowl until a thick paste forms. Scoop the paste into a small plastic bag, cut a tiny hole in one corner of the bag, and squeeze the paste to form the letter "B" on the top of the cake.

And put it in the oven for baby and me!

Put the cake into the oven and bake until golden brown, about 17 to 20 minutes. Using oven mitts, remove the baking tray from the oven and let the cake cool for 30 minutes before slicing it "for baby and me."

THIS IS THE WAY WE MAKE
OUR LUNCH...

THREE BLIND MICE
Mouse Tail Chicken Nuggets

❀

MARY, MARY, QUIET CONTRARY
Cockle Shell Pasta Salad

❀

HICKORY DICKORY DOCK
Hickory BBQ Pizza Clock

❀

THE OLD WOMAN WHO LIVED IN A SHOE
Shoestring Chicken Noodle Soup

THREE BLIND MICE

MOUSE TAIL
CHICKEN NUGGETS

Makes Fourteen to Sixteen Nuggets

THIS RHYME NEEDS:

1 pound (454 g) ground chicken
1 teaspoon onion powder
½ teaspoon salt
1 cup (70 g) panko-style breadcrumbs
Fresh green beans, about 16

 Preheat oven to 400°F (200°C)

Three blind mice, three blind mice…

Put the chicken, onion powder, and salt into a large mixing bowl.

See how they run, see how they run…

Run your hands and fingers through the chicken and spices until everything is combined and the mixture feels smooth and sticky.

29

They all run after the farmer's wife...

Pour the breadcrumbs onto a plate. Scoop about 1 tablespoon of the chicken mixture into your hands, form it into a round nugget, and roll it in the breadcrumbs to coat.

Who cut off their tails with a carving knife...

Give the mice back their tails by pushing one green bean into the side of each chicken nugget. Place the nuggets on a nonstick baking tray and pat them slightly flat.

Did you ever see such a sight in your life, as three blind mice?

Place the tray in the oven and cook until the nuggets are golden brown, about 20 minutes. Have you ever tasted such a bite in your life as crunchy, munchy nugget mice?

MARY, MARY, QUITE CONTRARY

COCKLE SHELL PASTA SALAD

Serves Eight

THIS RHYME NEEDS:

1 pound (454 g) small shells pasta, cooked
3 tablespoons vegetable oil
3 tablespoons red wine vinegar
⅓ cup (50 g) chopped black olives
4 teaspoons seasoned salt
2 tablespoons water
½ cup (100 g) canned corn, drained
½ red bell pepper, chopped small
½ cup (75 g) frozen peas, thawed

Mary, Mary, quite contrary…

Pour the contrary oil and vinegar into a large mixing bowl.

How does your garden grow?

To grow your garden, put the black olives—the garden "dirt"—into the mixing bowl. Sprinkle in the seasoned salt, or the garden "seeds." Add the water and corn—the "sunshine"—and mix everything together.

33

With silver bells...

Put the chopped bell pepper into the bowl.

And cockle shells...

Add the cooked pasta shells to the bowl and stir until the pasta is mixed with the dressing and vegetables.

And pretty maids all in a row.

Place the peas—the "pretty maids"—in rows on top of the pasta. Cover the bowl and let the pasta salad cool in the refrigerator for at least 30 minutes before serving.

HICKORY DICKORY DOCK

HICKORY BBQ PIZZA CLOCK

Serves One

THIS RHYME NEEDS:

2 tablespoons hickory-flavored barbecue sauce
1 can (5 ounces / 142 g) chicken, drained
1 large flour tortilla
½ cup (45 g) Colby-Jack or other mild cheese
12 slices pepperoni
1 spring onion

 Preheat oven to 400°F (200°C)

Hickory, dickory, dock...

Put the hickory barbecue sauce and chicken into a bowl and stir them together.

The mouse ran up the clock...

Put the flour tortilla on a baking sheet, cover it with the barbecue chicken, sprinkle it with cheese, and lay 12 slices of pepperoni all around the crust, just like the twelve hours on a clock.

The clock struck one...

To make the hands of the clock, cut off two sprigs of the spring onion (just the green part) and lay them on the pizza—make sure they point to one o'clock!

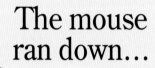

The mouse ran down...

Place the pizza clock down into the oven and let it bake for 10 minutes, or until the crust is brown and crispy.

Hickory, dickory, dock.

Using oven mitts, remove the baking tray from the oven and, with a pizza cutter, cut the pizza into four slices—one for hickory, one for dickory, one for dock...and one for you!

THE OLD WOMAN WHO LIVED IN A SHOE

SHOESTRING CHICKEN NOODLE SOUP

Serves Six

THIS RHYME NEEDS:

8 ounces (227 g) thin spaghetti
Baby carrots, about 12
1 pound (453 g) boneless, skinless chicken thighs, cut into small, bite-size pieces
8 cups (2 L) chicken broth
Crackers for soup, about 20

There was an old woman who lived in a shoe…

One small handful at a time, break each "shoestring" of spaghetti into four smaller pieces. Put the broken spaghetti into a large pot.

She had so many children, she didn't know what to do…

Cut the baby carrots into "so many" pieces, and put them into the pot with the spaghetti.

She gave them some broth without any bread…

Put the chicken pieces and broth into the pot. Cover the pot with a lid and place it on the stove over high heat. When the soup begins to boil, turn the heat to medium-low and cook until the noodles are tender, about 10 to 12 minutes.

And whipped them all soundly…

While you wait for the soup to cook, put the crackers into a resealable plastic bag. Close the bag tightly and smash the crackers until they turn into large crumbs.

And put them to bed.

Ladle the soup into bowls and top each bowl with a soft bed of cracker crumbs.

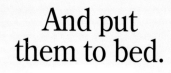

THIS IS THE WAY WE MAKE
OUR TREATS...

SING A SONG OF SIXPENCE
Blackberry Sandwich Pies

❋

HEY DIDDLE DIDDLE
Moon on a Spoon Candy Pops

❋

OLD MOTHER HUBBARD
Cheesy Dog Bone Snacks

❋

OLD KING COLE
Merry Berry Cider Bowl

SING A SONG OF SIXPENCE

BLACKBERRY SANDWICH PIES

Makes One Sandwich

THIS RHYME NEEDS:

1 large ripe banana
2 slices white sandwich bread
½ teaspoon chocolate-hazelnut spread
½ teaspoon blackberry jam
½ tablespoon melted butter

Preheat oven to 400°F (200°C)

Sing a song of sixpence…

Slice the banana into six round pieces.

A pocketful of rye…

Lay a slice of sandwich bread onto a cutting board and put one piece of banana in the middle of the slice. Squash the banana slightly onto the bread. If you like, use the remaining banana slices to make more sandwiches!

Four and twenty blackbirds…

Put the chocolate-hazelnut spread and blackberry jam onto the banana in the center of the bread. Using your finger, swirl together the chocolate and jam to slightly mix them.

Baked in a pie.

Lay another slice of bread directly over the first slice and, pressing down with a large cup, cut through both slices of bread to make a sandwich pie. Discard the leftover crust or save it for another use.

When the pie was opened the birds began to sing…

Using the tip of a small knife, make a little x-shaped opening on the top of the sandwich pie.

Wasn't that a dainty dish to set before the king?

Daintily brush the top of the sandwich pie with melted butter. Transfer the pie to a baking tray and put it in the oven for 7 minutes, or until the top is lightly golden. Using oven mitts, remove the pie from the oven and set it before the king!

49

HEY DIDDLE DIDDLE

MOON ON A SPOON
CANDY POPS

Makes Ten

THIS RHYME NEEDS:

2 cups (60 g) crispy rice cereal
1 cup (190 g) creamy peanut butter
1 cup (18 g) white chocolate chips
1 tablespoon chocolate sprinkles
10 plastic spoons

Hey diddle diddle…

Put the rice cereal, or "hay," and peanut butter into a large bowl, and mix with a spoon, or clean hands, until well combined. Chill the mixture in the freezer for 30 minutes.

The cat and the fiddle…

Once the mixture is chilled, put the white chocolate chips and chocolate sprinkles, or the "cat whiskers," into a coffee mug. Heat in the microwave in 30-second intervals until the chocolate is melted. Stir well.

The cow jumped over the moon…

Take the peanut butter mixture out of the freezer and shape it into 10 round, moon-shaped balls.

The little dog laughed to see such fun…

What fun! Use your fingers to quickly dip each peanut butter ball into the mug of melted chocolate, then place each ball onto a plastic spoon.

And the dish ran away with the spoon.

Place the spoons on a shallow dish or plate and "run it away" into the freezer for 15 minutes, or until the chocolate is hard and ready to eat.

OLD MOTHER HUBBARD

....

CHEESY DOG BONE SNACKS

(FOR HUMANS)

Makes Ten

THIS RHYME NEEDS:

¼ cup (40 g) all-purpose flour
2 tablespoons (28 g) butter, softened to room temperature
1 cup (90 g) finely-shredded sharp cheddar cheese
Parchment paper

 Preheat oven to 350˚F (180˚C)

Old Mother Hubbard
went to the cupboard...

Go to your cupboard and fetch all the ingredients. Put the flour, butter, and cheese into a large mixing bowl and mix them together with your hands until they form a dough.

To fetch her poor
dog a bone.

Shape the dough into dog bones: First roll out 10 strips of dough about the size of a grown-up finger (3-inches long and ½-inch wide) and place them on a parchment-lined baking tray. Next, make two small balls of dough for the ends of each strip and press them gently into place.

But when she got there the cupboard was bare...

Put the baking tray of dog bones inside your bare oven and bake them for 12 to 15 minutes, or until the bones are golden and crispy.

And so the poor dog had none.

Not anymore! You'll have lots of bones for your cupboard now. Remove the tray from the oven, using mitts, and let them cool on the tray before snacking.

OLD KING COLE

MERRY BERRY CIDER BOWL

Makes Four Cups

THIS RHYME NEEDS:

2 cups (500 ml) unfiltered apple juice
2 cups (500 ml) cranberry juice cocktail
1 banana, peeled
½ navel orange
3 cinnamon sticks

Old King Cole was a merry old soul and a merry old soul was he…

Pour the apple juice and "merry berry" cranberry juice into a medium pot.

He called for his pipe...

Put the whole banana into the pot.

And he called for his bowl...

Squeeze the juice of half a navel orange into the pot, then let the squeezed orange half— the "bowl"—float in the pot.

And he called for his fiddlers three.

Add three cinnamon sticks—the "fiddlers"—to the pot.

Oh there's none so rare, as can compare, with King Cole and his fiddlers three.

 Set the pot on the stove over high heat, bring the cider to a boil, cover the pot, turn off the heat, and let the cider rest for 20 minutes. Drink the cider warm or cold—Old King Cole likes both.

THIS IS THE WAY WE MAKE
OUR SWEETS...

LITTLE MISS MUFFET
Curds-and-Whey Ice Cream

❋

LITTLE JACK HORNER
Plum Crumble Pie

❋

LITTLE BO-PEEP
Lost Sheep Popsicles

❋

JACK AND JILL
Pail of Cotton-Crown Water

LITTLE MISS MUFFET

CURDS-AND-WHEY ICE CREAM

Serves Four

THIS RHYME NEEDS:

7 ounces (198 g) marshmallow fluff

1 carton (16 ounces / 453 g)
"no salt added" cottage cheese

½ cup (95 g) mini semi-sweet chocolate chips

Little Miss Muffet sat on a tuffet…

Put the marshmallow fluff—the "tuffet"—into a food processor.

Eating her curds and whey…

Put the cottage cheese into the processor. Blend until the mixture is perfectly smooth.

When along came a spider that sat down beside her...

Pour the mixture into a freezer-safe bowl and stir in the chocolate chips, or the "spiders."

And frightened Miss Muffet away.

Away the bowl goes into the freezer until the ice cream is frightfully frozen. Then find the nearest tuffet and enjoy it like little Miss Muffet.

LITTLE JACK HORNER

PLUM CRUMBLE PIE

Serves Six

THIS RHYME NEEDS:

2 cups (170 g) old-fashioned oats
1 box (9 ounces / 255 g) yellow cake mix
1 stick (113 g) unsalted butter, melted
Non-stick cooking spray
4 plums, cut into large chunks
1 tablespoon sugar

 Preheat oven to 350°F (180°C)

Little Jack Horner sat in a corner…

Put the oats and cake mix into a large mixing bowl.
Pour the melted butter into one side of the mixture (that's where Jack sits!)
and mix everything together to make a crumbly dough.

Eating a Christmas pie.

Spray a 9-inch (23 cm) pie
pan with nonstick cooking
spray, and put half of the
dough into the pie pan.

He put in his thumb...

Using your thumbs and fingers, press the dough into the bottom of the pie pan to make one thin layer of crust.

And pulled out a plum...

Put the chopped plums and sugar into a mixing bowl and gently stir them together. Pour the sugared plums into the pie pan, on top of the crust, and spread them out in one even layer.

And said,
"What a good boy am I!"

Sprinkle the remaining half of the dough over the plums and put the pie into the oven for 40 minutes, or until the top is slightly brown. But remember: don't stick your thumb into hot pies! Let the pie cool before eating.

LITTLE BO-PEEP

LOST SHEEP POPSICLES

Makes Fourteen

THIS RHYME NEEDS:

2 cups (85 g) mini marshmallows
2 (5.3-ounce / 150 g) containers strawberry yogurt
1 ice-cube tray
14 Popsicle sticks

Little Bo-Peep has lost her sheep…

Put the marshmallows—the "little sheep"—into a mixing bowl. Spoon the strawberry yogurt into the bowl and mix everything together until the sheep are "lost" in the yogurt.

And can't tell where to find them.

Spoon the yogurt mixture evenly into the empty ice-cube tray. Poke a Popsicle stick straight into the center of each cube.

Leave them alone,
and they'll come home...

*Put the Popsicles into the freezer and leave them alone
until fully frozen, about 3 to 4 hours.*

Wagging their tails behind them.

When frozen, wag the ice-cube tray from side to side to loosen the Popsicles from the tray. Tug on the sticks to pull each Popsicle out of the tray, and then lick your way to the little lost sheep.

JACK AND JILL

PAIL OF
COTTON-CROWN WATER

Serves Two

THIS RHYME NEEDS:

1 cup (250 ml) seltzer water
1 cup (250 ml) white grape juice
Cotton candy, about 1 cup (20 g)
2 maraschino cherries

Jack and Jill went up the hill...

Put a handful of ice cubes—a "small hill"—into two drinking glasses.

To fetch a pail of water...

Pour ½ cup seltzer water and ½ cup grape juice over the ice in each glass.

Jack fell down and broke his crown...

Break off a small ball of cotton candy (about ½ cup) and push it down into each glass until dissolved.

And Jill came tumbling after.

Tumble a maraschino cherry into each glass, stir it, and fetch a sip.

ABOUT THE AUTHOR

Bryan Kozlowski is the author of *Cook Me a Story* and a graduate of The Culinary Institute of America. A lover of classic and children's literature, he has been published in *The New York Times, Slate,* and *Country Life* magazine.